I. Introduction

Merger policy in the industrialized countries is largely motivated by classical theories of oligopoly whose roots trace to the theories developed by Cournot (1838) and Bertrand (1883).[1] The Merger Guidelines in the U.S., for example, rely heavily on modern variants of these theories, which predict that a merger between competitors with market power can raise prices significantly unless the merger generates offsetting efficiencies or attracts sufficient post-merger entry.[2] Unfortunately, however, the classical theories and their progeny generally make no distinction between final good and intermediate-goods markets. The theories assume that firms set take-it or leave-it prices that apply to all buyers, which is a reasonable assumption for most final-goods markets and some intermediate-goods markets, but it is not descriptive of pricing in many intermediate-goods markets.

A common feature of pricing in manufacturing sectors is that contracts are negotiated with individual downstream firms. For example, manufacturers of products sold through retail outlets like supermarkets, convenience stores, and mass merchants often negotiate different contracts with each distributor. Moreover, these contracts are a far cry from the simple, linear price set unilaterally by firms in the classical theories. The payment schedules one observes in reality are often highly nonlinear, with features like slotting fees, minimum quantity thresholds, and quantity discounts. They may also involve variants of bundling, such as aggregate rebates and full-line forcing.

In this paper we incorporate nonlinear supply contracts, bargaining and bundling (defined as inter-dependent price schedules) into a model of upstream competition to examine the effects of horizontal mergers. We focus on the simplest market setting in which these factors are present: $N \geq 2$ upstream manufacturers and a single downstream retailer, with no uncertainty, no asymmetric information, and no moral hazard. We find that the effects of horizontal mergers in this simple environment differ substantially from the effects predicted by the classical theories of oligopoly.

[1] See the 1992 Horizontal Merger Guidelines, at http://www.ftc.gov/bc/docs/horizmer.htm. The unilateral effects section of the Guidelines discusses markets in which the firms are distinguished by their capacities, and markets in which they are distinguished by product differentiation. The former is motivated by Cournot's model of oligopoly among producers of homogeneous products, while the latter is motivated by Bertrand competition among producers of differentiated products. The coordinated effects section of the Guidelines follows closely the ideas in Stigler's (1964) theory of oligopoly, which is understood today as a repeated game among Cournot or Bertrand competitors.

[2] See Deneckere and Davidson (1985), Farrell and Shapiro (1990), and the discussion in Willig (1991).

One key difference between an environment in which firms distribute their products through a common retailer and an environment in which firms sell their products directly to consumers is that, in the former environment, all pricing externalities can be internalized. As Bernheim and Whinston (1985; 1998) and O'Brien and Shaffer (1997) have shown, when two single-product firms make take-it-or-leave-it offers to a common retailer, the supply contracts yield the vertically-integrated outcome (maximize overall joint profit). In this paper we show that this result also holds under simultaneous Nash bargaining for the case of $N \geq 2$ single-product firms, and for the case of N firms selling single or multiple products *if* the multi-product firms can bundle their products.

This has surprising implications for merger policy. If bundling is feasible, it means that a merger between two single-product firms that sell differentiated products to a common retailer need not have any effect on input choices, output choices, wholesale prices, or final-goods prices. Thus, in contrast to conventional wisdom, a merger between upstream competitors with significant market power need not lead to higher prices even if there are no offsetting cost efficiencies or post-merger entry. In this environment, the U.S. Merger Guidelines fail to offer much in the way of guidance. Nor is it be possible to deduce appropriate public policy based on whether the buyer (retailer) feels it would benefit or be harmed. The merging firms would have an incentive to merge even absent cost savings because the combined entity would be able to extract more surplus from the retailer. Although the retailer would oppose the merger, consumer and total welfare would be unchanged.

Things are more complicated if bundling is not feasible (or is prohibited). In that case, the effect of a merger on final-goods prices, and hence on consumer and total welfare, depends on the relative bargaining powers of the merged firm and the retailer, as measured by their bargaining weights in an asymmetric Nash bargaining solution. If the merged firm's bargaining power is low enough, post-merger contracts are efficient and the welfare effects are the same as in the case with bundling: welfare is higher if there are cost-efficiencies related to the merger, and otherwise there is no change. But if the merged firm's bargaining power is sufficiently high, the merged firm no longer has an incentive to negotiate an efficient contract. This contrasts with what one might expect from models of common agency. However, it has a simple, intuitive interpretation. When bundling is not feasible, the distortion arises because the retailer can credibly threaten to drop one of the merged firm's products if the merged firm attempts to extract more than the incremental surplus generated by each product. In this case, the merged firm does better negotiating *higher* than efficient marginal transfer prices. Although this allows the firm to extract more surplus than it would otherwise obtain (because it reduces the retailer's profit from dropping one of its products), it also tends to reduce total welfare. Unless there are offsetting efficiencies, the merger would unambiguously lead to higher prices. Thus, when post-merger bundling is not feasible and the merged firm's bargaining power is sufficiently high, the qualitative tradeoffs of mergers predicted by the classical theories of oligopoly re-emerge.

In addition to its implications for mergers, our model has implications for the on-going policy debate over the use of "bundled discounts" by multi-product firms. Several high-profile cases in Europe involving vitamins, tires, and soft drinks have hinged on the alleged use of these discounts by larger firms to exclude smaller rivals.[3] To satisfy the EC Commission, for example, Cola Cola Export was forced to remove from its contracts with large distributors any rebates that were conditioned on the buyer's purchases of other beverages in addition to its purchases of *Coca Cola*. Bundled discounts are sometimes viewed skeptically by antitrust authorities because they may raise barriers to entry, allowing the larger firm to charge higher prices.[4] However, in our setting bundled discounts can lead to lower transfer prices if the bundling firm's bargaining power with respect to the retailer is high enough. Thus, a policy of prohibiting bundled discounts can lead to higher final-goods prices and lower welfare if it fails to induce offsetting entry. Prohibiting such discounts might also make mergers less profitable, preventing efficient mergers from taking place. A complete assessment of the effects of bundled discounts requires balancing the potential static benefits we identify against the potential dynamic effects on entry and exit.

The literature on mergers in intermediate-goods markets is surprisingly sparse. The seminal

---

[3]See *Hoffman-La Roche v EC Commission* [1979] European Commmission Report 461, at p. 547 (para. 111), *Michelin v EC Commission* [1983] European Commission Report 3461, at pp. 3520-3522 (para. 92-99), and *Coca Cola Export Corporation, Filiale Italiana*, Commission press release IP (88), 615 of 13 October 1988.

[4]Similar concerns have been expressed in the U.S. by Tom, Balto, and Averitt (2000). There are also private litigation cases. Recently, a major supplier of hospital beds and burial caskets got sued for bundling discounts on standard hospital beds to purchases of its specialty hospital beds. The parties agreed to an out-of-court settlement.

work in this area is Horn and Wolinsky (1988), who use the Nash bargaining solution to analyze incentives for mergers in markets where competing downstream firms acquire inputs from independent suppliers, and in which they acquire inputs from a monopoly supplier. Horn and Wolinsky differ from us in that their upstream suppliers do not compete, bargaining takes place over linear prices only, and the inputs are assumed to be homogeneous. von Ungern-Sternberg (1996) and Dobson and Waterson (1997) also use the Nash bargaining solution to analyze the effects of mergers on input prices. They too, however, restrict attention to linear prices and do not consider bundling. The market structure they consider consists of a single upstream firm. Other papers in this area look at different market structures, do not allow for bargaining, and do not consider bundling.[5]

Much of the literature on multiproduct pricing focuses on the use of bundling to extract surplus from heterogeneous buyers (Adams and Yellen, 1976; McAfee, et al. 1989; Mathewson and Winter, 1997) or to leverage monopoly power across markets (Whinston, 1990; Choi and Stefanadis, 2001; and Carlton and Waldman, 2002). In contrast, bundling is profitable in our model even when there is a single buyer (the downstream retail monopolist) and no opportunity to leverage across markets. Bundling also takes place with substitute goods in our model, in contrast to the well-studied cases of bundling with independent or complementary goods. The closest paper to ours in the literature on multiproduct pricing is Shaffer (1991), who considers bundling in a bilateral monopoly setting with take-it-or-leave-it offers. However, his model does not allow for upstream rivalry, mergers, or bargaining, nor does he consider the welfare implications of a policy prohibiting bundling.

The remainder of the paper is organized as follows. Section II presents the model and solves for the pre-merger equilibrium. Section III solves for the post-merger equilibrium and discusses output and welfare effects with and without bundling. Section IV examines the profit effects of mergers and explores the effects of cost savings. Section V discusses extensions and concludes the paper.

[5]Ziss (1995) considers mergers-to-monopoly in a market setting with two manufacturer-retailer pairs. Colangelo (1995) looks at pre-emptive mergers. Neither considers bundling because each firm sells only one product.

II. The Model and Pre-Merger Equilibria

$N \geq 2$ upstream firms (manufacturers) each distribute a single differentiated product through a downstream monopolist.[6] Manufacturer i's production cost is $C_i(q_i) \geq 0$, where $C_i(0) = 0$ and $q_i \geq 0$ is the quantity it produces. The downstream firm (retailer) resells the manufacturers' products to final consumers. Its net revenue from selling $\mathbf{q} \equiv (q_1, q_2, ..., q_N)$ units, after subtracting all costs other than what it pays the manufacturers, is $R(\mathbf{q})$. We assume that $R(\mathbf{q}) - \sum_i C_i(q_i)$ is concave and differentiable for all $q_i > 0$, and that it has a unique maximum at $\mathbf{q^I} \equiv (q_1^I, q_2^I, ..., q_N^I)$. We refer to the quantity vector $\mathbf{q^I}$ and associated joint profit as "the fully-integrated outcome."

Competitive interactions are modelled as a two-stage game. In stage one, the manufacturers simultaneously negotiate contracts with the retailer over the price of their products. In stage two, with all contracts in place, the retailer decides how much of each product to buy, and hence how much to resell to final consumers. As in Horn and Wolinsky (1988), we assume the outcomes of bargaining are determined by the set of simultaneous, asymmetric Nash bargaining solutions between the retailer and each manufacturer. In the event a negotiation breaks down, each firm in the negotiation earns its disagreement payoff. For the manufacturer, who has only the retailer as a trading partner, we normalize this payoff to zero. In the case of the retailer, we assume its disagreement payoff with each manufacturer is the profit it could earn without that manufacturer.[7]

Manufacturer i's contract with the retailer is a function $T_i(\cdot)$, which specifies the retailer's payment for any quantity q_i purchased. We assume $T_i(0) = 0$ and $T_i(q_i) \geq C_i(q_i)$ for all q_i. Additional restrictions on contracts are discussed as needed. This formulation permits most contractual forms observed in practice, including linear wholesale prices, two-part tariffs, and quantity forcing. It does not permit payments to depend on final-goods prices (resale price maintenance), or on the retailer's purchases of other manufacturers' products (e.g., we do not allow exclusive dealing provisions).

[6] Many of our results go through with $M > 2$ retailers if the retailers do not observe each others' contracts and have passive beliefs (O'Brien and Shaffer, 1992; McAfee and Schwartz, 1994). This is discussed further in section V.

[7] The simultaneous Nash bargaining solution also arises in the literature on labor market negotiations, which are analogous to negotiations between upstream and downstream firms. For example, Davidson (1988) considers bargaining between a union and two employers, and Jun (1989) examines bargaining between two unions and one or two employers. These papers show that the simultaneous Nash bargaining solution is equivalent to perfect equilibria of natural alternating offer bargaining games in the limit as the time between offers goes to zero.

We now characterize the bargaining equilibrium. Given the vector of contracts $\mathbf{T} \equiv (T_1(\cdot), T_2(\cdot), ..., T_N(\cdot))$, the retailer chooses quantities to maximize profits. Let $\Omega(\mathbf{T})$ be the set of quantity vectors that maximize the retailer's profit given the contract vector $\mathbf{T}$. That is,

$$\Omega(\mathbf{T}) \equiv \arg\max_{\mathbf{q}} R(\mathbf{q}) - \sum_j T_j(q_j).$$

In the first stage, the retailer and each manufacturer negotiate their contract recognizing that the retailer will subsequently choose quantities from the set $\Omega(\mathbf{T})$. Let $\mathbf{T_{-i}}$ denote the vector of contracts of firm i's rivals, e.g., $\mathbf{T_{-1}} \equiv (T_2(\cdot), T_3(\cdot), ..., T_N(\cdot))$. Then, given $\mathbf{T_{-i}}$, we can define the feasible set of quantity-contract combinations available to manufacturer i and the retailer as

$$\mathcal{A}_i(\mathbf{T_{-i}}) \equiv \{(q_i, T_i(\cdot)) \mid \mathbf{q} \in \Omega(\mathbf{T}), T_i(0) = 0, T_i(q_i) \geq C_i(q_i)\}.$$

Thus, the Nash bargaining solution between manufacturer i and the retailer solves

$$\max_{(q_i, T_i(\cdot)) \in \mathcal{A}_i(\mathbf{T_{-i}})} (\pi_i - d_i)^{\alpha_i} (\pi_r - d_{r_i})^{1-\alpha_i} \tag{1}$$

where $\pi_i = T_i(q_i) - C_i(q_i)$ is manufacturer i's profit; $\pi_r = R(\mathbf{q}) - \sum_j T_j(q_j)$ is the retailer's profit; d_i and d_{r_i} are the disagreement profits of manufacturer i and the retailer, respectively; and $\alpha_i \in [0, 1]$ is manufacturer i's bargaining weight. As discussed previously, the disagreement profit for manufacturer i is $d_i = 0$. The disagreement profit of the retailer with manufacturer i is

$$d_{r_i} = \max_{\mathbf{q_{-i}}} R(0, \mathbf{q_{-i}}) - \sum_{j \neq i} T_j(q_j),$$

where, for ease of exposition, we use $R(0, \mathbf{q_{-i}})$ in place of $R(q_1, ..., q_{i-1}, 0, q_{i+1}, ..., q_N)$.

A *bargaining equilibrium* is a set of quantities and contracts that solve (1) for each product i. We refer to an equilibrium in which K products are sold as"K-product" equilibria, $K \in \{1, 2, ..., N\}$.

Characterization of equilibrium quantities and payoffs

Unfortunately, the maximization problem in (1) is not easy to work with because it involves the choice of a function $T_i(\cdot)$ and hence it is not amenable to calculus. However, as we show below, we can nevertheless characterize equilibrium quantities and payoffs by solving an equivalent problem in which manufacturer i and the retailer choose a quantity-forcing contract with two parameters,

$$T_i^F(q_i) = \begin{cases} 0 & \text{if } q_i = 0 \\ F_i & \text{if } q_i = q_i' \\ \infty & \text{otherwise} \end{cases},$$

and quantity q_i, from the feasible set of quantity-contract combinations

$$\mathcal{A}_i^F(\mathbf{T_{-i}}) \equiv \{(q_i, F_i, q_i') \mid \mathbf{q} \in \arg\max_{\mathbf{q}} R(\mathbf{q}) - T_i^F(q_i) - \sum_{j\neq i} T_j(q_j),\ F_i \geq C_i(q_i')\}.$$

With this restriction to quantity-forcing contracts, the maximization problem in (1) becomes

$$\max_{(q_i,F_i,q_i')\in\mathcal{A}_i^F(\mathbf{T_{-i}})} \left(T_i^F(q_i) - C_i(q_i)\right)^{\alpha_i} \left(R(\mathbf{q}) - T_i^F(q_i) - \sum_{j\neq i} T_j(q_j) - d_{r_i}\right)^{1-\alpha_i}. \tag{2}$$

We will henceforth assume the Nash product in (2) has a unique solution. Then Lemma 1 below implies that the solution to (2) yields the same quantities and payoffs as any solution to (1).

Lemma 1 *Suppose* $(\hat{q}_i, \hat{F}_i, \hat{q}_i') \in \mathcal{A}_i^F(\mathbf{T}^*_{\mathbf{-i}})$ *is the unique solution to the maximization problem in (2) given the vector of rival contracts* $\mathbf{T}^*_{\mathbf{-i}}$*. Suppose* $(q_i^*, T_i^*(\cdot)) \in \mathcal{A}_i(\mathbf{T}^*_{\mathbf{-i}})$ *is a solution to the maximization problem in (1) given the vector of rival contracts* $\mathbf{T}^*_{\mathbf{-i}}$*. Then* $\hat{q}_i = q_i^*$ *and* $\hat{F}_i = T_i^*(q_i^*)$*.*

Proof: Suppose $(q_i^*, T_i^*(\cdot)) \in \mathcal{A}_i(\mathbf{T}^*_{\mathbf{-i}})$ is a solution to (1) given the vector of contracts $\mathbf{T}^*_{\mathbf{-i}}$, and let $\mathbf{q}^* \in \Omega(\mathbf{T}^*)$. Note that $\mathcal{A}_i^F(\mathbf{T_{-i}}) \subset \mathcal{A}_i(\mathbf{T_{-i}})$, and that the quantities $\mathbf{q}^*$ and payments $T_j^*(q_j^*)$ can be obtained when quantity-contract combinations are restricted to the set $\mathcal{A}_i^F(\mathbf{T}^*_{\mathbf{-i}})$ by setting $q_i = q_i^*$, $F_i = T_i^*(q_i^*)$, and $q_i' = q_i^*$. Thus, $(q_i^*, T_i^*(q_i^*), q_i^*) \in \mathcal{A}_i^F(\mathbf{T}^*_{\mathbf{-i}})$ solves the maximization problem in (2) for manufacturer i and the retailer, and the two maximization problems yield the same quantities and payoffs for manufacturer i and the retailer, conditional on contracts $\mathbf{T}^*_{\mathbf{-i}}$. **Q.E.D.**

Suppose $(\mathbf{q}^*, \mathbf{T}^*)$ is a vector of quantities and contracts that form a bargaining equilibrium, where $\mathbf{q}^* \equiv (q_1^*, ..., q_N^*)$ and $\mathbf{T}^* \equiv (T_1^*, ..., T_N^*)$. Then Lemma 1 implies that we can characterize the equilibrium quantity and payoffs for manufacturer i and the retailer by solving the problem:[8]

$$\begin{aligned} &\max_{(q_i,F_i,q_i')\in\mathcal{A}_i^F(\mathbf{T}^*_{\mathbf{-i}})} (F_i - C_i(q_i))^{\alpha_i} \left(R(\mathbf{q}) - F_i - \sum_{j\neq i} T_j^*(q_j) - d_{r_i}\right)^{(1-\alpha_i)} \\ &= \max_{q_i,F_i,\mathbf{q_{-i}}} (F_i - C_i(q_i))^{\alpha_i} \left(R(\mathbf{q}) - F_i - \sum_{j\neq i} T_j^*(q_j) - d_{r_i}\right)^{(1-\alpha_i)} \end{aligned} \tag{3}$$

[8]Note that this does not imply that the forcing contracts that solve the restricted problem and the contracts $\mathbf{T}^*_{\mathbf{-i}}$ form a bargaining equilibrium because the best responses of rivals to the forcing contract T_i^F may differ from $\mathbf{T}^*_{\mathbf{-i}}$. The appeal to forcing contracts is only a means to characterize the bargaining equilibrium quantities and profits.

such that

$$F_i \geq C_i(q_i), \tag{4}$$

$$R(\mathbf{q}) - F_i - \sum_{j \neq i} T_j^*(q_j) \geq d_{r_i}, \tag{5}$$

where constraints (4) and (5) ensure that manufacturer i and the retailer earn at least their disagreement profits. The equality in (3) follows because the constraint $(q_i, F_i, q_i') \in \mathcal{A}_i^F(\mathbf{T}^*_{-\mathbf{i}})$ requires that $\mathbf{q_{-i}}$ maximize $R(\mathbf{q}) - \sum_{j \neq i} T_j^*(q_j)$. Since $F_i - C_i(q_i)$ is independent of $\mathbf{q_{-i}}$, and F_i and d_{r_i} are fixed when the retailer chooses $\mathbf{q_{-i}}$, this amounts to choosing $\mathbf{q_{-i}}$ to maximize the Nash product.

The first-order conditions for F_i and q_i at an interior solution of (3) are

$$\alpha_i \pi_i^{(\alpha_i - 1)} (\pi_r - d_{r_i})^{(1-\alpha_i)} - (1 - \alpha_i)\pi_i^{\alpha_i} (\pi_r - d_{r_i})^{-\alpha_i} = 0. \tag{6}$$

$$-C_i'(q_i)\alpha_i \pi_i^{(\alpha_i - 1)} (\pi_r - d_{r_i})^{(1-\alpha_i)} + \frac{\partial R(\mathbf{q})}{\partial q_i}(1 - \alpha_i)\pi_i^{\alpha_i} (\pi_r - d_{r_i})^{-\alpha_i} = 0. \tag{7}$$

Substituting (6) into (7) and simplifying yields

$$\frac{\partial R(\mathbf{q})}{\partial q_i} - C_i'(q_i) = 0, \tag{8}$$

which implies that q_i^* maximizes the joint profit of manufacturer i and the retailer given $\mathbf{T}^*_{-\mathbf{i}}$. Since this must be true for all i, the bargaining equilibrium quantities must maximize overall joint profits, i.e., $q_i^* = q_i^I$, provided (3) has an interior solution for each i. This proves the following proposition.

Proposition 1 *All N-product bargaining equilibria replicate the fully-integrated outcome.*

Proposition 1 extends to bargaining with N upstream firms the well-known result in the agency literature that a common retailer internalizes all pricing externalities when manufacturers make take-it-or-leave-it offers, and thus that marginal transfer pricing is efficient (Bernheim and Whinston, 1985). This has an intuitive interpretation. Fix the contracts of all manufacturers other than i, and consider negotiations between the retailer and manufacturer i. Since nonlinear contracts are feasible, they will choose their quantity to maximize their bilateral profits and divide the surplus with a non-distortional transfer. Note that choosing q_i to maximize their bilateral profits, $R(\mathbf{q}) - \sum_{j \neq i} T_j^*(q_j) - C_i(q_i)$, is the same as choosing q_i to maximize overall joint profit.

III. Post-merger Equilibria and Output Effects

Suppose manufacturers 1 and 2 merge. This alters negotiations in potentially three ways. First, it affects the retailer's disagreement profit with the merged firm. After the merger, the retailer's disagreement profit is the profit it would earn if it did not sell products 1 *and* 2. Second, it may affect the retailer's bargaining power. After the merger, the retailer's bargaining weight in the Nash bargaining solution with respect to the newly merged firm, $\alpha_m \in [0, 1]$, may differ from what it was with respect to each firm separately. Third, it affects the contracts the merged firm may be able to negotiate. After the merger, contracts in which the payments for q_1 and q_2 are interdependent may be feasible. We say that the merged firm engages in *bundling* if the payment for one of its products depends on the amount purchased of the other. Formally, let $T_m(q_1, q_2)$ be the merged firm's contract with the retailer, where q_1 is the quantity the retailer purchases of product 1 and q_2 is the quantity the retailer purchases of product 2. Then $T_m(q_1, q_2)$ exhibits bundling if and only if there does *not* exist $T_1(q_1)$ and $T_2(q_2)$ such that $T_m(q_1, q_2) = T_1(q_1) + T_2(q_2)$ for all $q_1, q_2 \geq 0$.

A. Mergers with Bundling

Let $C_m(q_1, q_2)$ be the post-merger cost of producing q_1 units of product 1 and q_2 units of product 2. We say that the merger generates cost efficiencies at quantities (q_1, q_2) if and only if $C_m(q_1, q_2) < C_1(q_1) + C_2(q_2)$. If there are no cost savings at (q_1, q_2), then $C_m(q_1, q_2) = C_1(q_1) + C_2(q_2)$.

Let π_m denote the merged firm's post-merger profit. Then $\pi_m = T_m(q_1, q_2) - C_m(q_1, q_2)$. As before, the retailer will choose quantities from the set $\Omega(\mathbf{T})$ in stage two, where $\mathbf{T}$ now equals $(T_m(\cdot, \cdot), T_3(\cdot), ..., T_N(\cdot))$. Thus, given the rivals' contracts, $\mathbf{T_{-1,2}} \equiv (T_3(\cdot), ..., T_N(\cdot))$, we can define the feasible set of quantity-contract combinations available to the merged firm and retailer as

$$\mathcal{A}_m(\mathbf{T_{-1,2}}) \equiv \{(q_1, q_2, T_m(\cdot, \cdot)) \mid \mathbf{q} \in \Omega(\mathbf{T}), T_m(0, 0) = 0, T_m(q_1, q_2) \geq C_m(q_1, q_2)\}.$$

The feasible set of quantity-contract combinations available to rival firm j is still $\mathcal{A}_j(\mathbf{T_{-j}})$.

Suppose $\mathbf{q^B} \equiv (q_1^B, ..., q_N^B)$ and $\mathbf{T^B} \equiv (T_m^B, T_3^B, ..., T_N^B)$ form a bargaining equilibrium when bundling is feasible. Then the Nash bargaining solution between the merged firm and retailer solves

$$\max_{(q_1,q_2,T_m(\cdot,\cdot))\in\mathcal{A}_m(\mathbf{T}^{\mathbf{B}}_{-\mathbf{1},\mathbf{2}})} (\pi_m - d_m)^{\alpha_m} (\pi_r - d_{r_m})^{(1-\alpha_m)}, \tag{9}$$

where d_m and d_{r_m} are the disagreement profits of the merged firm and retailer. The disagreement profit of the merged firm is $d_m = 0$. The disagreement profit of the retailer with the merged firm is

$$d_{r_m} = \max_{\mathbf{q}_{-\mathbf{1},\mathbf{2}}} R(0,0,\mathbf{q}_{-\mathbf{1},\mathbf{2}}) - \sum_{j\neq 1,2} T_j(q_j).$$

Characterization of equilibrium quantities and payoffs

We can use the same method that we used in the previous section to characterize equilibrium quantities and payoffs. In particular, let $T^F_m(\cdot,\cdot)$ be a quantity-forcing contract with $T^F_m(0,0) = 0$, $T^F_m(q_1', q_2') = F_m$, and $T^F_m(q_1, q_2) = \infty$ otherwise. Then, as we show in the appendix, we can characterize the equilibrium quantities and payoffs for the merged firm and retailer by solving

$$\max_{q_1,q_2,F_m,\mathbf{q}_{-\mathbf{1},\mathbf{2}}} (F_m - C_m(q_1,q_2))^{\alpha_m} \left(R(\mathbf{q}) - F_m - \sum_{j\neq 1,2} T^B_j(q_j) - d_{r_m} \right)^{(1-\alpha_m)} \tag{10}$$

such that

$$F_m \geq C_m(q_1, q_2), \tag{11}$$

$$R(\mathbf{q}) - F_m - \sum_{j\neq 1,2} T^B_j(q_j) \geq d_{r_m}. \tag{12}$$

where constraints (11) and (12) ensure that the merged firm and retailer earn at least their disagreement profits when q_1, $q_2 > 0$. The constraints that the retailer would rather choose q_1, $q_2 > 0$ than $q_1 = 0$, $q_2 > 0$, or $q_1 > 0$, $q_2 = 0$, are not binding because $T^F_m(q_1, q_2)$ in these cases equals ∞.

The first-order conditions for F_m and q_i at an interior solution of (10) are

$$\alpha_m \pi_m^{(\alpha_m - 1)} (\pi_r - d_{r_m})^{(1-\alpha_m)} - (1-\alpha_m)\pi_m^{\alpha_m} (\pi_r - d_{r_m})^{-\alpha_m} = 0. \tag{13}$$

$$-\frac{\partial C_m(q_1,q_2)}{\partial q_i} \alpha_m \pi_m^{(\alpha_m-1)} (\pi_r - d_{r_m})^{(1-\alpha_m)} + \frac{\partial R(\mathbf{q})}{\partial q_i}(1-\alpha_m)\pi_m^{\alpha_m} (\pi_r - d_{r_m})^{-\alpha_m} = 0. \tag{14}$$

Substituting (13) into (14) and simplifying yields

$$\frac{\partial R(\mathbf{q})}{\partial q_i} - \frac{\partial C_m(q_1,q_2)}{\partial q_i} = 0, \tag{15}$$

which implies that q_i^B maximizes the joint profit of the merged firm and retailer given $\mathbf{T^B_{-1,2}}$. Since this must be true for $i = 1, 2$, and since rival manufacturers solve the same problem as before (prior to the merger), it must be that the bargaining equilibrium quantities maximize overall joint profit, i.e., $q_j^B = q_j^I$, provided (3) and (10) have interior solutions. This proves the following proposition.

Proposition 2 *Suppose manufacturers* 1 *and* 2 *merge. Then, if the merged firm can bundle its products, the fully-integrated outcome is realized in all N-product bargaining equilibria.*

Proposition 2 extends the common-agency result to the case of N firms selling one or more products to a common retailer *if* the multi-product firms can bundle their products. It implies, among other things, that a merger between upstream competitors with market power need not lead to higher prices for consumers even if there are no offsetting cost efficiencies. In the absence of cost efficiencies, we see from Propositions 1 and 2 that a merger between two upstream rivals will have no effect on input choices, output choices, wholesale prices, or final-goods prices. These results are surprising because they differ substantially from the effects of mergers that arise in the classical theories of oligopoly. Perhaps the biggest difference is the diminished role of concentration indices and cross elasticities in our model as predictors of the competitive effects of a merger. For example, if bundling is feasible, a merger without cost savings is benign regardless of the degree of market power in the upstream market or the degree of substitution between the merging firms' products. In these instances, the U.S. Merger guidelines fail to offer much in the way of guidance.

B. Mergers without Bundling

Suppose bundling is not feasible. Then the merged firm and retailer must negotiate a contract that is additively separable in q_1 and q_2, i.e., $T_m(q_1, q_2) = T_1(q_1) + T_2(q_2)$. Recall that $T_i^F(0) = 0$, $T_i^F(q_i') = F_i$, and $T_i^F(q_i) = \infty$ otherwise. Suppose $\mathbf{q^{NB}} \equiv (q_1^{NB}, ..., q_N^{NB})$ and $\mathbf{T^{NB}} \equiv (T_1^{NB}, ..., T_N^{NB})$ form a bargaining equilibrium when bundling is infeasible. Then, as we show in the appendix, we can characterize the equilibrium quantities and payoffs for the merged firm and retailer by solving

$$\max_{q_1,q_2,F_1,F_2,\mathbf{q_{-1,2}}} (F_1 + F_2 - C_m(q_1, q_2))^{\alpha_m} \left(R(\mathbf{q}) - F_1 - F_2 - \sum_{j \neq 1,2} T_j^{NB}(q_j) - d_{r_m} \right)^{(1-\alpha_m)} \quad (16)$$

such that

$$F_1 + F_2 \geq C_m(q_1, q_2), \tag{17}$$

$$R(\mathbf{q}) - F_1 - F_2 - \sum_{j\neq 1,2} T_j^{NB}(q_j) \geq d_{r_m}, \tag{18}$$

$$R(\mathbf{q}) - F_1 - F_2 - \sum_{j\neq 1,2} T_j^{NB}(q_j) \geq \max_{q_2,\mathbf{q_{-1,2}}} R(0, q_2, \mathbf{q_{-1,2}}) - T_2^F(q_2) - \sum_{j\neq 1,2} T_j^{NB}(q_j), \tag{19}$$

$$R(\mathbf{q}) - F_1 - F_2 - \sum_{j\neq 1,2} T_j^{NB}(q_j) \geq \max_{q_1,\mathbf{q_{-1,2}}} R(q_1, 0, \mathbf{q_{-1,2}}) - T_1^F(q_1) - \sum_{j\neq 1,2} T_j^{NB}(q_j), \tag{20}$$

where constraints (17) and (18) ensure that the merged firm and retailer earn at least their disagreement profits when q_1, $q_2 > 0$. Constraints (19) and (20) are individual rationality constraints that ensure that the retailer earns weakly higher profit by choosing q_1, $q_2 > 0$ than by dropping product 1 (constraint 19) or product 2 (constraint 20). The right-hand sides of (19) and (20) are weakly larger than the right-hand side of (18). With bundling, these constraints are always satisfied because in these cases $T_m^F(\cdot, \cdot) = \infty$. Without bundling, however, these constraints may bind.

Lemma 2 *There exists $\overline{\alpha}_m \in (0, 1)$ such that for all $\alpha_m > \overline{\alpha}_m$ constraints (19) and (20) bind.*

Proof: See the appendix.

Lemma 2 says that if the manufacturer's bargaining weight is sufficiently high, (19) and (20) must bind in any N-product bargaining equilibrium. To see this intuitively, suppose the merged firm had all the bargaining power ($\alpha_m = 1$). If constraints (19) or (20) did not bind, the merged firm would raise one of the fixed fees to the point where the retailer earns its disagreement profit $d_{r_m} = \max_{\mathbf{q_{-1,2}}} R(0, 0, \mathbf{q_{-1,2}}) - \sum_{j\neq 1,2} T_j^{NB}(q_j)$. Since d_{r_m} is weakly smaller than the right-hand sides of (19) and (20), this contradicts the assumption that one of the constraints does not bind.

When the constraints do not bind ($\alpha_m < \overline{\alpha}_m$), the problem in (16) is equivalent to the problem in (10) with $F_m = F_1 + F_2$. In this case, bargaining without bundling yields the fully-integrated outcome. When the constraints bind ($\alpha_m > \overline{\alpha}_m$), the equilibrium quantities for the merged firm and retailer can be found by substituting the binding constraints into (16). For convenience, define

$$v_1(q_1) = \max_{\mathbf{q_{-1,2}}} R(q_1, 0, \mathbf{q_{-1,2}}) - F_1 - \sum_{j\neq 1,2} T_j^{NB}(q_j), \tag{21}$$

$$v_2(q_2) = \max_{\mathbf{q_{-1,2}}} R(0, q_2, \mathbf{q_{-1,2}}) - F_2 - \sum_{j \neq 1,2} T_j^{NB}(q_j). \tag{22}$$

The function $v_i(q_i)$ is the profit of the retailer if it purchases product i but drops product j. Substituting these definitions into constraints (19) and (20), and then substituting the constraints into the objective in (16), the merged firm and retailer's maximization problem becomes

$$\max_{q_1, q_2} \left(R(\mathbf{q}) - \frac{v_1(q_1) + v_2(q_2)}{2} - \sum_{j \neq 1,2} T_j^{NB}(q_j) - C_m(q_1, q_2) \right)^{\alpha_m} \left(\frac{v_1(q_1) + v_2(q_2)}{2} - d_{r_m} \right)^{(1-\alpha_m)}. \tag{23}$$

To gain insight into the solution, assume that $T_j^{NB}(q_j)$ is continuously differentiable (i.e., $v_1(q_1)$ and $v_2(q_2)$ are differentiable). After some algebra, the first-order condition for q_1 can be written as

$$\frac{\partial R(\mathbf{q})}{\partial q_1} - \frac{\partial C_m(q_1, q_2)}{\partial q_1} = \frac{1}{2} \left[1 - \frac{(1-\alpha_m)\pi_m}{\alpha_m(\pi_r - d_{r_m})} \right] \frac{\partial v_1(q_1)}{\partial q_1}. \tag{24}$$

A symmetric condition holds for q_2. The term on the left-hand side of (24) is the derivative of overall joint profit with respect to q_1. Since profits are concave and single-peaked, this derivative equals zero at the fully-integrated outcome, exceeds zero if $q_1^{NB} < q_1^I$, and is less than zero if $q_1^{NB} > q_1^I$. The term in square brackets on the right-hand side of (24) is positive. This is true because when the constraints (19) and (20) bind, the merged firm receives less than its "fair share" of the profits from Nash bargaining, i.e., $(1-\alpha_m)\pi_m < \alpha_m(\pi_r - d_{r_m})$. Therefore, the sign of $\frac{\partial R(\mathbf{q})}{\partial q_1} - \frac{\partial C_m(q_1,q_2)}{\partial q_1}$ is the same as the sign of $\frac{\partial v_1(q_1)}{\partial q_1}$. Using the envelope theorem, the derivative of $v_1(q_1)$ is

$$\frac{\partial v_1(q_1)}{\partial q_1} = \frac{\partial R(q_1, 0, \tilde{\mathbf{q}}_{\mathbf{-1,2}}(q_1))}{\partial q_1} > 0. \tag{25}$$

where $\tilde{\mathbf{q}}_{\mathbf{-1,2}}(q_1) \equiv \arg\max_{\mathbf{q_{-1,2}}} R(q_1, 0, \mathbf{q_{-1,2}}) - \sum_{j \neq 1,2} T^{NB}(q_j)$. Therefore, at the bargaining equilibrium, $\frac{\partial R(\mathbf{q})}{\partial q_1} - \frac{\partial C_m(q_1,q_2)}{\partial q_1} > 0$, which implies that $q_1^{NB} < q_1^I$. An analogous argument implies that $q_2^{NB} < q_2^I$. This proves Proposition 3 for the case in which $T_j^{NB}(q_j)$ is continuously differentiable.

Proposition 3 *Suppose manufacturers 1 and 2 merge. If the merged firm cannot bundle its products, then whether or not the fully-integrated outcome is realized depends on α_m: (i) if $\alpha_m < \overline{\alpha}_m$, the fully-integrated outcome is obtained in all N-product bargaining equilibria; (ii) if $\alpha_m > \overline{\alpha}_m$, the merged firm distorts its quantities downward and the fully-integrated outcome is not obtained.*

Proof: See the appendix for the case in which $T_j^{NB}(q_j)$ is not continuously differentiable.

Proposition 3 contains the main result of the paper. It says that if the merged firm's bargaining weight *vis a vis* the retailer is sufficiently low, then the constraints (19) and (20) do not bind and the incentives of the two firms are to maximize bilateral joint profit. However, if the merged firm has a lot of bargaining power ($\alpha_m > \overline{\alpha}_m$), then maximizing bilateral joint profit is not optimal because the negotiated F_1 and F_2 will be constrained by the ability of the retailer to drop one or both of the products. For example, if the merged firm attempts to extract 'too much' surplus by raising F_1, then the retailer can drop product 1 (constraint (19) is violated), and similarly, product 2 will be dropped if the merged firm attempts to extract 'too much' surplus by raising F_2 (constraint (20) is violated). To relax these constraints, it is optimal for the merged firm to induce an upward distortion in its input pricing (decrease its quantities) in order to decrease the retailer's payoff. By reducing the retailer's quantity of product 2, for example, the retailer is harmed in the event it sells products 1 and 2, but it would be harmed even more if it were to drop product 1 (because products are substitutes). The former is a second-order effect while the latter is a first-order effect.

This result is surprising because it contrasts with the common intuition that overall joint profits tend to be maximized in situations of common agency and complete information. We have shown that this intuition does not necessarily extend to a negotiations setting in which the upstream firm has sufficiently high bargaining power. In that case, the merged firm (or any multiproduct firm) will find it optimal to knowingly reduce the overall profit pie because in doing so it can capture a larger share for itself. With a larger share of a smaller pie, the manufacturer can gain.

Our results have implications for the output and welfare effects of mergers. They imply that a merger without bundling either does not affect output ($\alpha_m < \overline{\alpha}_m$) or causes the merged firms' outputs to fall ($\alpha_m > \overline{\alpha}_m$). In the former case the post-merger contracts are efficient and the welfare effects are the same as in the case with bundling: welfare is higher if there are efficiencies related to the merger, and otherwise there is no change. In the latter case, the merged firm no longer has an incentive to negotiate an efficient contract, and welfare would typically fall. Because the goods are substitutes, rival firms would respond by increasing their quantities, but typically not by enough to offset the negative welfare effect of the reduction in the merged firms' quantities.

Our results also have implications for policy toward bundled discounts. If the bargaining power of the merged firm is high enough, prohibiting bundling leads to higher marginal transfer prices for the merged firm's products. Any attempt by authorities to prevent a multi-product firm from increasing its "clout" through bundling may therefore result in higher prices for final consumers. This finding suggests that antitrust concerns with bundling by dominant, multiproduct firms may be misguided unless there is reason to believe that bundling has foreclosed, or is likely to foreclose rivals. In our model bundling arises not to foreclose rivals but to extract rent from the retailer.

IV. Profit Effects

Expressions for equilibrium profits can be derived for each case by solving the restricted (quantity-forcing) negotiations of each firm for its optimal fixed fee and then substituting back into the expressions for profits. The resulting equilibrium profit expressions for the pre-merger case are

$$\pi_i^* = \alpha_i \left(R(\mathbf{q^I}) - C_i(q_i^I) - \sum_{j \neq i} T^*(q_j^I) - d_{r_i}^* \right), \quad i = 1, ..., N \tag{26}$$

$$\pi_r^* = R(\mathbf{q^I}) - \sum_i C_i(q_i^I) - \sum_i \pi_i^* \tag{27}$$

$$d_{r_i}^* = \max_{\mathbf{q_{-i}}} R(0, \mathbf{q_{-i}}) - \sum_{j \neq i} T_j^*(q_j)$$

where π_i^* is manufacturer i's equilibrium profit, π_r^* is the retailer's equilibrium profit, and $d_{r_i}^*$ is the retailer's disagreement profit with manufacturer i under the equilibrium contracts $T_j^*(\cdot)$, $\forall j \neq i$.

Notice that manufacturer i's profits are expressed in terms of rival firms' equilibrium contracts and not just in terms of the revenue and cost primitives. This is because the contracts are not uniquely determined in equilibrium. The reason for this is that there are many different contracts for product j that induce the retailer to select a given quantity q_j^*, and the disagreement profit of the retailer in negotiations with firm i depend on the contract with firm j at quantities other than q_j^*. Thus, firm i's equilibrium profits depend on the type of equilibrium contracts employed by rival firms $j \neq i$. The non-uniqueness of profits means that it is not possible to compare pre-merger and post-merger profits at this level of generality. Further restrictions are needed to make this comparison. In the remainder of this section we restrict attention to two-part tariff contracts, and we assume that the manufacturers have constant marginal costs, i.e., $C_i''(q_i) = 0$, $i = 1, ..., N$.

Before proceeding we need some more notation. Let $w_i^I = C_i'(q_i)$, $i = 1, ..., N$, be the constant per-unit prices (wholesale prices) that yield the vertically-integrated outcome. Define

$$\Pi \equiv R(\mathbf{q^I}) - \sum_i w_i^I q_i^I, \tag{28}$$

$$\Pi_{-i} \equiv \max_{\mathbf{q_{-i}}} R(0, \mathbf{q_{-i}}) - \sum_{j \neq i} w_j^I q_j, \tag{29}$$

$$\Pi_{-1,2} \equiv \max_{\mathbf{q_{-1,2}}} R(0, 0, \mathbf{q_{-1,2}}) - \sum_{k \neq 1,2} w_k^I q_k. \tag{30}$$

These are the retailer's maximized profits (net of fixed fees) if it sells all N products, all but product i, and all but products 1 and 2, respectively, when its marginal costs are given by w_i^I, $i = 1, ..., N$.

A. Profit Effects with No Cost Savings

Using (26) and the definitions (28)-(30), manufacturer i's pre-merger profit under two-part tariffs is

$$\pi_i^* = \alpha_i \left(R(\mathbf{q^I}) - C_i(q_i^I) - \sum_{j \neq i} w_j^I q_j^I - \Pi_{-i} \right). \tag{31}$$

The profit of the merged firm when it bundles its products can be found by solving the first-order conditions for (10) and then substituting them into the expression for profit. This gives

$$\pi_m^B = \alpha_m \left(R(\mathbf{q^I}) - C_m(q_1^I, q_2^I) - \sum_{j \neq 1,2} w_j^I q_j^I - \Pi_{-1,2} \right). \tag{32}$$

Suppose the merger does not increase the manufacturers' bargaining power or affect their costs ($C_m(q_1, q_2) = C_1(q_1) + C_2(q_2)$). Then the benefit to manufacturers 1 and 2 from merging is

$$\begin{aligned} \Delta\pi_m^B &= \pi_m^B - \pi_1^* - \pi_2^* \\ &= \alpha_m \left([\Pi - \Pi_{-1,2}] - [\Pi - \Pi_{-1}] - [\Pi - \Pi_{-2}] \right). \end{aligned} \tag{33}$$

The term $\Pi - \Pi_{-1,2}$ is the cost to the retailer (net of fixed fees) of failing to reach an agreement with the merged firm. The term $\Pi - \Pi_{-i}$, $i \in \{1, 2\}$, is the cost to the retailer of failing to reach an agreement with manufacturer i prior to the merger. Equation (33) indicates that the merger will be profitable if the expression in parenthesis is positive, i.e., if the retailer's cost of failing to reach an agreement with the merged firm is greater than the sum of the costs of failing to reach agreement with of each of the merging firms prior to the merger. This is intuitive. A manufacturer's bargaining strength comes in part from its ability to inflict a loss on the retailer by refusing an agreement. If the loss imposed by the merged firm exceeds the sum of the losses imposed by the merging firms prior to the merger, then the merged firm will extract greater rents from the retailer. In general, the concavity of joint profits ensures that this will be the case. Since the products are substitutes, the loss imposed by the merged firm will indeed exceed the sum of the losses imposed by the merging firms prior to the merger (see the proof of Proposition 4 below).[9] Thus, we have that $\Delta\pi_m^B > 0$, implying that mergers are profitable for the merging firms when bundling is feasible.

Next we consider the profitability of a merger when bundling is infeasible. If the merged firm's bargaining weight is less than $\overline{\alpha}_m$, then the constraints (19) and (20) do not bind and the maximization problem in (16) is the same as the maximization problem in (10) with $F_m = F_1 + F_2$. In this case, the merger is profitable and the profit of the merged firm is the same with or without bundling. However, if $\alpha_m > \overline{\alpha}_m$, then at the integrated quantities the merged firm is constrained from capturing its share of the incremental profits from its products. That is, an unconstrained Nash bargaining solution would require $(1 - \alpha_m)\pi_m = \alpha_m(\pi_r - d_{r_m})$, but constraints (19) and (20) force $(1 - \alpha_m)\pi_m < \alpha_m(\pi_r - d_{r_m})$. This establishes an upper bound on π_m. Since the wholesale price of each non-merging firm is unchanged whether or not bundling is feasible, it follows that the merged firm is worse off when $\alpha_m > \overline{\alpha}_m$ and bundling is infeasible than when bundling is feasible.

To determine whether the merger itself is profitable when bundling is infeasible and $\alpha_m > \overline{\alpha}_m$, let π_m^{NB} denote the profit of the merged firm in this case. Then, using the fact that the constraints (19) and (20) will bind in any bargaining equilibrium, and that when $\alpha_m > \overline{\alpha}_m$ the merged firm prefers to introduce a distortion by inducing the retailer to choose the vector of quantities $\mathbf{q}^{\mathbf{NB}}$ in

[9] Inderst and Wey (2003;14) also obtain this result, in a different context, using the Shapley value as their solution concept to multilateral bargaining. As they note, "Broadly speaking, a merger shifts bargaining away from the margin. If the created net surplus is smaller at the margin ... the respective market side prefers to become integrated."

equilibrium rather than $\mathbf{q^I}$, it can be shown that (see the proof of Proposition 4 below)

$$\pi_m^{NB} > \sum_{i=1,2}\left(R(\mathbf{q^I}) - \sum_{j\neq i} w_j^I q_j^I - \Pi_{-i}\right) - C_m(q_1^I, q_2^I). \tag{34}$$

Assuming, as before, that the merger does not affect relative bargaining weights or the merged firm's costs ($C_m(q_1, q_2) = C_1(q_1) + C_2(q_2)$), the benefit to manufacturers 1 and 2 from merging is

$$\begin{aligned}\Delta\pi_m^{NB} &= \pi_m^{NB} - \pi_1^* - \pi_2^* \\ &> \sum_{i=1,2}(1-\alpha_i)\left(R(\mathbf{q^I}) - C_i(q_i^I) - \sum_{j\neq i} w_j^I q_j^I - \Pi_{-i}\right),\end{aligned} \tag{35}$$

which is positive if pre-merger profits are positive and $\alpha_i < 1$. Intuitively, the merger is profitable even when the manufacturer is constrained for two reasons. First, the merged firm's fixed fees rise to the point where constraints (19) and (20) bind, whereas they do not bind prior to the merger unless $\alpha_i = 1$. Second, the merged firm earns additional profit by reducing its output of each product (raising its wholesale price) in order to capture more profit from selling the other product.

We summarize these results for the bundling and no-bundling cases in the following proposition.

Proposition 4 *A merger between manufacturers 1 and 2 is profitable whether or not bundling is feasible, even if there are no cost-savings from the merger and no increase in their collective bargaining weight. If $\alpha_m < \overline{\alpha}_m$, then the merged firm's profits are the same with and without bundling. If $\alpha_m > \overline{\alpha}_m$, then the merged firm's profit is higher with bundling than without bundling.*

Proof: See the appendix.

The result that mergers are always profitable in our model even if there are no cost savings contrasts with the results in the standard models of horizontal mergers in final-goods markets where the profitability of a merger often turns on whether the firms' strategies are strategic substitutes or strategic complements. In the latter case, we know from Deneckere and Davidson (1985) and others that mergers of any size are profitable because, in addition to the usual gains from coordination, they induce less aggressive pricing by the non-merging firms. In the former case, however, we know from Salant et al. (1983) and others that, in the absence of cost savings, mergers may not be profitable because they induce rival firms to respond by increasing their outputs. In our model, mergers are profitable even without cost savings because (a) they allow the merging firms to impose losses on the retailer by jointly withholding their products, and (b) the non-merging firms' wholesale prices do not change pre and post merger (that is, the rival firms do not respond aggessively).

Effects on the Non-merging Firms' Profits

Next, consider the effects of a merger on the non-merging firms' profits. The nature of the bargaining problem between these firms and the retailer does not change after the merger. A non-merging firm's profit in any regime has the same structure as (31) but is evaluated at the wholesale prices and quantities corresponding to the particular regime. In all the efficient regimes—pre-merger, post-merger with bundling, and post-merger with no bundling and $\alpha_m < \overline{\alpha}_m$—the wholesale prices and quantities are the same. A non-merging firm's profits are the same across these regimes.

In the post-merger regime with no bundling and $\alpha_m > \overline{\alpha}_m$, the merged firm reduces its outputs by raising its wholesale prices above the fully-integrated prices. To see the effect of this on rival firms, let $\mathbf{q^e}(w_1, w_2) \equiv (q_1^e(w_1, w_2), ..., q_N^e(w_1, w_2))$ denote the vector of bargaining equilibrium quantities, where $q_j^e(w_1, w_2)$ is the bargaining equilibrium quantity of product j when the merged firm has wholesale prices w_1 and w_2. Then we can write a non-merging firm i's profit as

$$\begin{aligned} \pi_i &= \alpha_i(R(\mathbf{q^e}(w_1, w_2)) - C_i(q_i^e(w_1, w_2)) \\ &- w_1 q_1^e(w_1, w_2) - w_2 q_2^e(w_1, w_2) - \sum_{j \neq 1,2,i} w_j^I q_j^e(w_1, w_2) \\ &- \max_{\mathbf{q_{-i}}}[R(0, \mathbf{q_{-i}}) - w_1 q_1 - w_2 q_2 - \sum_{j \neq 1,2,i} w_j^I q_j]), \end{aligned} \tag{36}$$

where we have substituted w_j^I for w_j, $j \neq 1, 2, i$, because the wholesale prices of each non-merging firm equals marginal cost in any bargaining equilibrium. Let $\tilde{q}_j(w_1, w_2)$, for all $j \neq i$, solve the maximization problem in the third line of (36). Then, using the envelope theorem, we have

$$\frac{\partial \pi_i}{\partial w_1} = \alpha_i(\tilde{q}_1(w_1, w_2) - q_1^e(w_1, w_2)). \tag{37}$$

Since $\tilde{q}_j(w_1, w_2) - q_j^e(w_1, w_2) > 0$ for all j when the products are substitutes, it follows that a non-merging firm i's profit will be increasing in w_1. A symmetric argument implies that a non-merging firm i's profit will be increasing in w_2. Since w_1 and w_2 both rise after the merger if $\alpha_m > \overline{\alpha}_m$ and bundling is infeasible, the non-merging firms will benefit from the merger in this case.

Proposition 5 *A merger between manufacturers 1 and 2 that generates no cost savings has no effect on the non-merging firms' profits if bundling is feasible or if the merged firm's bargaining power is sufficiently low ($\alpha_m < \overline{\alpha}_m$). However, the same merger raises the non-merging firms' profits if bundling is infeasible and the merged firm's bargaining power is high ($\alpha_m > \overline{\alpha}_m$).*

Proposition 5 implies that the non-merging firms will oppose bundling by a merged firm when the merged firm has a lot of 'clout' *vis a vis* the retailer. However, we know from Proposition 3 that prohibiting bundling in this case leads to higher wholesale prices (lower outputs) and thus such opposition does not necessarily coincide with the interests of social welfare. When bundling is allowed, Proposition 5 implies that the non-merging firms will be indifferent to the merger.

Effects on the Retailer's Profit

Lastly, consider the effects of the merger on the retailer when there are no cost savings. Proposition 4 implies that the merging firms always benefit from the merger, and Proposition 5 implies that the non-merging firms either benefit or are not affected. Since overall joint profits are maximized pre-merger, it follows that the retailer is harmed by the merger if there are no cost savings.

We can also rank the retailer's preferences over bundling versus no bundling in the post-merger regime. The two cases can be nested by writing (19) and (20) for the no-bundling regime as

$$\pi_r \geq \max_{q_2,\mathbf{q_{-1,2}}} R(0, q_2, \mathbf{q_{-1,2}}) - T_2^F(q_1) - \sum_{j \neq 1,2} T_j^{NB}(q_j) - b, \tag{38}$$

$$\pi_r \geq \max_{q_1,\mathbf{q_{-1,2}}} R(q_1, 0, \mathbf{q_{-1,2}}) - T_1^F(q_1) - \sum_{j \neq 1,2} T_j^{NB}(q_j) - b. \tag{39}$$

In constraints (38) and (39), b is a parameter that represents the tightness of the constraints. The no-bundling case occurs when $b = 0$. The bundling case occurs when b is large enough that the constraints (38) and (39) do not bind. The effects of prohibiting bundling on the retailer can be found by evaluating the derivative of π_r with respect to b starting from the value of b at which the constraints just begin to bind.[10] As we show in the appendix, we find that the derivative is negative at this point, implying that the retailer is typically worse off under bundling than it is with no bundling. Mathematically, tightening the no-bundling constraint (decreasing b) has a first-order positive effect on the retailer's profits, as shown in (38) and (39). It also has a second-order effect that comes through equilibrium adjustments in wholesale prices and quantities as the bundling constraint is tightened. However, the second-order effects are outweighed by the first-order effects.

Proposition 6 *A merger between manufacturers 1 and 2 reduces the retailer's profit if there are no cost savings from the merger. If $\alpha_m < \overline{\alpha}_m$, then the retailer's profit is the same with and without bundling. If $\alpha_m > \overline{\alpha}_m$, then the retailer's profit is lower with bundling than without bundling.*

Proof: See the appendix.

As in the previous case with the non-merging firms, we would expect the retailer to oppose bundling by a merged firm when the latter has a lot of 'clout' vis a vis the retailer. However, as we have seen, such opposition does not necessarily coincide with the interests of social welfare. Whether or not bundling is allowed, Proposition 6 implies that we should expect the retailer to oppose any merger that does not generate cost savings. But this opposition is driven solely by the retailer's desire to preserve its profit; such a merger need not have any social welfare consequences.

B. Profit Effects with Cost Savings

To investigate the effects of cost savings from a merger between manufacturers 1 and 2, we rewrite the merged firm's costs as $C_m(q_1, q_2; \theta)$, where θ is a cost-shift parameter on the merged firm's products. Assume $\frac{\partial C_m(q_1,q_2;\theta)}{\partial \theta} > 0$, $\frac{\partial^2 C_m(q_1,q_2;\theta)}{\partial q_i \partial \theta} \geq 0$, and $\frac{\partial^2 C_m(q_1,q_2;\theta)}{\partial q_i^2} = 0$. An increase in θ increases the total cost and may increase the marginal cost of producing product i.

In the regimes where joint profits are maximized, the merged firm's profit can be written as

$$\pi_m = \alpha_m \left[R(\mathbf{q^I}) - C_m(q_1^I, q_2^I; \theta) - \sum_{j \neq 1,2} w_j^I q_j^I - \max_{\mathbf{q_{-1,2}}} [R(0, 0, \mathbf{q_{-1,2}}) - \sum_{j \neq 1,2} w_j^I q_j] \right] \quad (40)$$

[10] Note that either both constraints bind or neither constraint binds. If only one constraint was binding, the merged firm could adjust F_1 and F_2 to raise $F_1 + F_2$ and at the same time relax the binding constraint.

Differentiating the expression in (40) with respect to θ and using the envelope theorem gives

$$\frac{\partial \pi_m}{\partial \theta} = -\alpha_m \frac{\partial C_m(q_1^I, q_2^I; \theta)}{\partial \theta} \tag{41}$$

Since $\frac{\partial C_m(q_1,q_2;\theta)}{\partial \theta} > 0$ by assumption, condition (41) implies that $\frac{\partial \pi_m}{\partial \theta} < 0$. Thus the merged firm benefits from cost savings, whether the cost savings are fixed or marginal. The retailer will also benefit in this case because Nash bargaining will allow it to share in the cost savings.

The effects of the merged firm's cost savings on the non-merging firms' profits depend on whether the cost savings reduce fixed or marginal costs. Marginal-cost savings will have the same effect on profits as a reduction in w_1, as expressed in (37), and therefore will reduce the non-merging firms' profits. Fixed cost savings, on the other hand, do not affect the non-merging firms' profits.

It can be shown that cost savings in the no-bundling regime with $\alpha_m > \overline{\alpha}_m$ have the same qualitative effects. The retailer benefits from fixed and marginal cost savings; non-merging firms are harmed when the savings reduce the merged firm's marginal costs and are not affected otherwise.

Proposition 7 *Suppose the merger between manufacturers 1 and 2 reduces its costs. Fixed-cost reductions benefit the merged firm and the retailer and do not affect the non-merging firms. Marginal-cost reductions benefit the merged firm and the retailer and harm the non-merging firms.*

In this model, the merged firm's outputs increase if and only if its marginal costs decrease. It follows that the merger harms the non-merging firms if and only if it reduces the merging firms' marginal costs. Since the merged firm extracts greater rents from the retailer, the merger will still harm the retailer if the cost savings are small. Thus, in this model the preferences of the non-merging firms are an indicator of the output effects of a merger, while the preferences of the retailer may be misleading.

V. Conclusion

A phrase often used by business people in explaining the reasons for a merger is that it will increase the merged firm's 'clout' in negotiations with buyers or suppliers. As such, antitrust investigations of upstream mergers in intermediate-goods markets often focus on the effects of the merger on the combined entity's bargaining strength *vis a vis* the customer, and whether the customer will be harmed as a result.[11] In this paper, additional clout may come from three sources: bargaining power, as measured by a firm's bargaining weight in its asymmetric Nash bargaining solution; the ability to negotiate contracts on products jointly rather than separately; and the ability to bundle products via interdependent price schedules, for example, by offering discounts and rebates that are applied 'across-the-board.'

We find that the merging firms may benefit from an increase in their clout even if it does not affect their marginal transfer prices. Absent cost savings, for the reasons noted above, mergers with bundling increase the merging firms' profits, decrease the retailer's profit, and leave rivals' profits unchanged. The profit effects are purely rent transfers; there is no effect on consumer or total welfare. In contrast, with cost savings, mergers with bundling increase the merging firms' profits and decrease rival firms' profits. If the cost savings are small, the retailer's share of the cost savings will be less than the rent transfer to the merged firm and the retailer's profit will decrease. Otherwise, if the cost savings are large enough, the retailer will gain. Thus, it is possible for the merger to increase welfare while harming both rival firms *and* the retailer, or just rival firms. Basing policy on the retailer's perceived benefit or harm is uninspired and uninformative in this case.

When bundling is not feasible, the increase in the merging firms' profits can be attributed to the benefits of negotiating terms on products jointly rather than separately. Because the products are substitutes, the loss imposed on the retailer by the merged firm if it withholds both products exceeds the sum of the losses that can be imposed by each merging firm prior to the merger. However, if the merged firm's bargaining power is high enough to induce it to raise wholesale prices, the benefits of merging are smaller than they are when bundling is allowed. Rival firms benefit if transfer prices increase, but the retailer is always worse off than with no merger, and worse off with bundling than without it after the merger if the merged firm's bargaining power is sufficiently high.

We view this paper as a first step toward understanding the effects of mergers in intermediate-

[11] See the European Commission Decision in Case No COMP/M.2220–General Electric/Honeywell, 2001, and In the Matter of Pepsi, Inc./Quaker Oats Company, Federal Trade Commission File No 0110059, August 1, 2001.

goods markets when contracts are negotiated. The model is too simple at this point to be definitive for policy conclusions. However, it is rich enough to show that the effects of mergers in this environment can be substantially different than the effects predicted by classical oligopoly models.

A simplification in this paper is the restriction to a single downstream firm. Under this assumption, equilibrium contracts are efficient (in the sense of replicating the fully-integrated outcome) before and after the merger except when bundling is prohibited and the merging firm's bargaining power is sufficiently high. This result has strong implications for the effects of mergers. If bundling is allowed, so that contracts are efficient before and after the merger, the merger increases the merged firm's output if and only if it reduces marginal costs. This result is independent of the degree of market power in the upstream market and the degree of substitution among upstream products. The merger also increases the merging firms' clout in negotiations with the retailer by increasing the combined loss the merging firms can impose by refusing to sell. An implication is that a merger with small cost savings enhances welfare even though it reduces the profits of rival firms *and* the retailer.

The obvious next step is to extend the model to an environment with downstream oligopoly. Once there is downstream competition, the rents to be split by a manufacturer and retailer will depend *inter-alia* on the amount of competition the retailer faces from rival retailers who sell the same product. In this case, contracts generally will not lead to the vertically-integrated outcome. An additional complication is that the nature of the equilibrium will depend on whether downstream firms can observe each others' contracts. If contracts are not observable, it can be shown that per-unit transfer prices will still equal marginal cost in a bargaining equilibrium. In this case, many of the results in this paper carry through. However, the implication that per-unit transfer prices equal marginal cost does not appear to be consistent with pricing in many intermediate-goods markets in which non-linear contracts are negotiated. If contracts are observable, then firms have incentives to negotiate contracts that dampen competition so as to increase the size of the total surplus to be split.[12] This generally leads to per-unit transfer prices that exceed marginal cost. The analysis of

[12]One factor that tends to make contracts more observable is the Robinson-Patman Act, which constrains the

mergers when contracts are observable among rivals is more complicated and awaits further work.

Another extension would be to allow for non-contractible investments by upstream or downstream firms. The need for ongoing, non-contractible investments in marketing or quality is another reason for upstream firms to earn positive economic margins, as one often observes in practice.

ability of manufacturers to price discriminate. See O'Brien and Shaffer (1994).

Appendix

Characterization of equilibrium quantities and payoffs with bundling

To characterize equilibrium quantities and payoffs, we solve an equivalent problem to the one in (9). In the equivalent problem, the merged firm and retailer choose a quantity-forcing contract

$$T_m^F(q_1, q_2) = \begin{cases} 0 & \text{if } q_1 = q_2 = 0 \\ F_m & \text{if } q_1 = q_1' \text{ and } q_2 = q_2' \\ \infty & \text{otherwise} \end{cases},$$

and quantities q_1 and q_2, from the feasible set of quantity-contract combinations

$$\mathcal{A}_m^F(\mathbf{T_{-1,2}}) \equiv \{(q_1, q_2, F_m, q_1', q_2') \mid \mathbf{q} \in \arg\max_{\mathbf{q}} R(\mathbf{q}) - T_m^F(q_1, q_2) - \sum_{j \neq 1,2} T_j(q_j), F_m \geq C_m(q_1', q_2')\}.$$

With this restriction to quantity-forcing contracts, the maximization problem in (9) becomes

$$\max_{(q_1,q_2,F_m,q_1',q_2') \in \mathcal{A}_m^F(\mathbf{T^B_{-1,2}})} \left(T_m^F(q_1, q_2) - C_m(q_1, q_2)\right)^{\alpha_i} \left(R(\mathbf{q}) - T_m^F(q_1, q_2) - \sum_{j \neq 1,2} T_j(q_j) - d_{r_m}\right)^{1-\alpha_i}. \tag{A.1}$$

We will henceforth assume that the Nash product in (A.1) has a unique solution. Then, since $\mathcal{A}_m^F(\mathbf{T_{-1,2}}) \subset \mathcal{A}_m(\mathbf{T_{-1,2}})$, and the choices $q_1' = q_1^B$, $q_2' = q_2^B$, and $F_m = T_m^B(q_1^B, q_2^B)$ are feasible when the merged firm and retailer choose a quantity-forcing contract, it follows that the solution to (A.1) yields the same quantities and payoffs for the merged firm and retailer as the solution to the problem in (9), conditional on contracts $\mathbf{T^B_{-1,2}}$. This means that we can characterize the equilibrium quantities and payoffs for the merged firm and retailer by solving the restricted problem:

$$\begin{aligned} &\max_{(q_1,q_2,F_m,q_1',q_2') \in \mathcal{A}_m^F(\mathbf{T^B_{-1,2}})} (F_m - C_m(q_1, q_2))^{\alpha_m} \left(R(\mathbf{q}) - F_m - \sum_{j \neq 1,2} T_j^B(q_j) - d_{r_m}\right)^{(1-\alpha_m)} \\ &= \max_{q_1,q_2,F_m,\mathbf{q_{-1,2}}} (F_m - C_m(q_1, q_2))^{\alpha_m} \left(R(\mathbf{q}) - F_m - \sum_{j \neq 1,2} T_j^B(q_j) - d_{r_m}\right)^{(1-\alpha_m)} \end{aligned} \tag{A.2}$$

such that

$$F_m \geq C_m(q_1, q_2),$$

$$R(\mathbf{q}) - F_m - \sum_{j \neq 1,2} T_j^B(q_j) \geq d_{r_m},$$

which correspond to (10)–(12), respectively. The rest follows from the discussion in the text.

Characterization of equilibrium quantities and payoffs without bundling

When bundling is not feasible, the merged firm and retailer must negotiate a contract that is additively separable in q_1 and q_2: $T_m(q_1, q_2) = T_1(q_1) + T_2(q_2)$. In this case, we define the feasible set of quantity-contract combinations available to the merged firm and retailer as

$$\hat{\mathcal{A}}_m(\mathbf{T_{-1,2}}) \equiv \{(q_1, q_2, T_1(\cdot), T_2(\cdot)) \mid \mathbf{q} \in \Omega(\mathbf{T}), T_1(0) + T_2(0) = 0, T_1(q_1) + T_2(q_2) \geq C_m(q_1, q_2)\}.$$

The feasible set of quantity-contract combinations available to rival firm j is still $\mathcal{A}_j(\mathbf{T_{-j}})$.

Suppose $(\mathbf{q^{NB}}, \mathbf{T^{NB}})$ form a bargaining equilibrium when bundling is infeasible. Then the Nash bargaining solution between the merged firm and retailer solves

$$\max_{(q_1,q_2,T_1(\cdot),T_2(\cdot)) \in \hat{\mathcal{A}}_m(\mathbf{T^{NB}_{-1,2}})} (\pi_m - d_m)^{\alpha_m}(\pi_r - d_{r_m})^{(1-\alpha_m)}. \tag{A.3}$$

Following the technique used to characterize the equilibrium in the bundling case, suppose that the merged firm and retailer restrict attention to a pair of quantity-forcing contracts in the set

$$\hat{\mathcal{A}}^F_m(\mathbf{T_{-1,2}}) \equiv \{(q_1, q_2, F_1, F_2, q_1', q_2') \mid \mathbf{q} \in \arg\max_{\mathbf{q}} R(\mathbf{q}) - \sum_{i=1,2} T_i^F(q_i) - \sum_{j \neq 1,2} T_j(q_j),$$
$$F_1 + F_2 \geq C_m(q_1', q_2')\}.$$

With this restriction to quantity-forcing contracts, the maximization problem in (A.3) becomes

$$\max_{(q_1,q_2,F_1,F_2,q_1',q_2') \in \hat{\mathcal{A}}^F_m(\mathbf{T^{NB}_{-1,2}})} \left(\sum_{i=1,2} T_i^F(q_i) - C_m(q_1, q_2)\right)^{\alpha_i} \left(R(\mathbf{q}) - \sum_{i=1,2} T_i^F(q_i) - \sum_{j \neq 1,2} T_j(q_j) - d_{r_m}\right)^{1-\alpha_i}. \tag{A.4}$$

We will henceforth assume that the Nash product in (A.4) has a unique solution. Then, since $\hat{\mathcal{A}}^F_m(\mathbf{T_{-1,2}}) \subset \hat{\mathcal{A}}_m(\mathbf{T_{-1,2}})$, and the choices $q_1' = q_1^{NB}$, $q_2' = q_2^{NB}$, $F_1 = T_1(q_1^{NB})$ and $F_2 = T_2(q_2^{NB})$ are feasible when the merged firm and retailer choose quantity-forcing contracts, it follows that the solution to (A.4) yields the same quantities and payoffs for the merged firm and retailer as the solution to (A.3), conditional on contracts $\mathbf{T^{NB}_{-1,2}}$. This means that we can characterize the equilibrium quantities and payoffs for the merged firm and retailer by solving the restricted problem:

$$\max_{(q_1,q_2,F_1,F_2,q_1',q_2')\in\hat{A}_m^F(\mathbf{T^{NB}_{-1,2}})} (F_1+F_2-C_m(q_1,q_2))^{\alpha_m}\left(R(\mathbf{q})-F_1-F_2-\sum_{j\neq 1,2} T_j^{NB}(q_j)-d_{r_m}\right)^{(1-\alpha_m)}$$

$$= \max_{q_1,q_2,F_1,F_2,\mathbf{q_{-1,2}}} (F_1+F_2-C_m(q_1,q_2))^{\alpha_m}\left(R(\mathbf{q})-F_1-F_2-\sum_{j\neq 1,2} T_j^{NB}(q_j)-d_{r_m}\right)^{(1-\alpha_m)} \quad \text{(A.5)}$$

such that

$$F_1+F_2 \geq C_m(q_1,q_2),$$

$$R(\mathbf{q})-F_1-F_2-\sum_{j\neq 1,2} T_j^{NB}(q_j) \geq d_{r_m},$$

$$R(\mathbf{q})-F_1-F_2-\sum_{j\neq 1,2} T_j^{NB}(q_j) \geq \max_{(q_2,\mathbf{q_{-1,2}})} R(0,q_2,\mathbf{q_{-1,2}})-T_2^F(q_2)-\sum_{j\neq 1,2} T_j^{NB}(q_j),$$

$$R(\mathbf{q})-F_1-F_2-\sum_{j\neq 1,2} T_j^{NB}(q_j) \geq \max_{(q_1,\mathbf{q_{-1,2}})} R(q_1,0,\mathbf{q_{-1,2}})-T_1^F(q_1)-\sum_{j\neq 1,2} T_j^{NB}(q_j),$$

which correspond to (16)–(20), respectively. The rest follows from the discussion in the text.

Proof of Lemma 2: Suppose (19) or (20) does not bind. Without loss of generality, let (19) be the non-binding constraint. Then the merged firm and retailer will negotiate F_1 to maximize the objective in (16). After some algebra, the first-order condition for F_1 can be written as

$$F_1+F_2 = \alpha_m(R(\mathbf{q})-\sum_{j\neq 1,2} T_j^{NB}(q_j)-d_{r_m})+(1-\alpha_m)C_m(q_1,q_2). \quad \text{(A.6)}$$

Substituting (A.6) into the expression for the retailer's profit gives

$$\begin{aligned}\pi_r &= R(\mathbf{q})-F_1-F_2-\sum_{j\neq 1,2} T_j^{NB}(q_j)\\ &= (1-\alpha_m)(R(\mathbf{q})-C_m(q_1,q_2)-\sum_{j\neq 1,2} T_j^{NB}(q_j))+\alpha_m d_{r_m}. \quad \text{(A.7)}\end{aligned}$$

Note that

$$\lim_{\alpha_m\to 1} \pi_r = d_{r_m} \quad \text{(A.8)}$$

Since (19) does not bind by assumption, condition (A.8) implies that for sufficiently large α_m,

$$d_{r_m} = \max_{\mathbf{q_{-1,2}}} R(0,0,\mathbf{q_{-1,2}})-\sum_{j\neq 1,2} T^{NB}(q_j)$$

$$> \max_{q_2, \mathbf{q_{-1,2}}} R(0, q_2, \mathbf{q_{-1,2}}) - T_2^F(q_2) - \sum_{j \neq 1,2} T_j^{NB}(q_j)$$

$$\geq \max_{\mathbf{q_{-1,2}}} R(0, 0, \mathbf{q_{-1,2}}) - T_2^F(0) - \sum_{j \neq 1,2} T^{NB}(q_j)$$

$$= \max_{\mathbf{q_{-1,2}}} R(0, 0, \mathbf{q_{-1,2}}) - \sum_{j \neq 1,2} T^{NB}(q_j),$$

which is a contradiction. **Q.E.D.**

Proof of Proposition 3: Assume that $T_j^{NB}(q_j)$ is differentiable almost everywhere. For convenience, we repeat conditions (21) and (22):

$$v_1(q_1) = \max_{\mathbf{q_{-1,2}}} R(q_1, 0, \mathbf{q_{-1,2}}) - F_1 - \sum_{j \neq 1,2} T^{NB}(q_j), \tag{A.9}$$

$$v_2(q_2) = \max_{\mathbf{q_{-1,2}}} R(0, q_2, \mathbf{q_{-1,2}}) - F_2 - \sum_{j \neq 1,2} T^{NB}(q_j). \tag{A.10}$$

Assume that the solutions to the maximization problems in (A.9) and (A.10) are unique.

The strategy of the proof is to show that even if the non-merging firms' contracts are not differentiable, the functions $v_i(\cdot)$, $i \in \{1, 2\}$, are differentiable at the equilibrium quantities and, in particular, condition (25) holds. The analysis presented in the text then establishes Proposition 3.

Let $\mathbf{q^1_{-1,2}}(q_1)$ solve the maximization problem in (A.9) and $\mathbf{q^2_{-1,2}}(q_2)$ solve the maximization problem in (A.10). Define

$$r_j^1(q_1, \mathbf{q_{-1,j}}) \equiv \arg\max_{q_j} R(q_1, 0, q_j, \mathbf{q_{-1,2,j}}) - F_1 - \sum_{j \neq 1,2} T^{NB}(q_j),\ j \in \{3, 4, ..., N\}. \tag{A.11}$$

The solution to the maximization problem in (A.9) can be characterized as the simultaneous solution to the $N-2$ "sub-maximization" problems in (A.11). Define $r_j^2(q_2, \mathbf{q_{-2,j}})$, $j \neq 1, 2$, symmetrically as the quantities that solve the analogous sub-maximization problems that correspond to (A.10).

Step 1. If $T_j^{NB}(q_j^{NB})$ is discontinuous in either direction from q_j^{NB}, it must jump upward; otherwise the retailer could increase its profits by choosing a different quantity.

Step 2. Suppose $T_j^{NB}(q_j^{NB})$ jumps up to both the right and the left of q_j^{NB}. Consider an arbitrarily small change in q_1^{NB} to $q_1^{NB} + x$. This will have an arbitrarily small effect on the marginal revenue of product j, so the solution to firm j's maximization problem in (A.11) will not change. That is, $r_j^1(q_1^{NB}, \mathbf{q_{-1,j}}) = r_j^1(q_1^{NB} + x, \mathbf{q_{-1,j}})$ provided that x is small. Similarly, $r_j^2(q_1^{NB}, \mathbf{q_{-2,j}}) = r_j^2(q_1^{NB} + x, \mathbf{q_{-2,j}})$ for small x.

Step 3. Suppose $T_j^{NB}(q_j)$ jumps up to the right of q_j^{NB}, but is continuous to the left. At the solution to (A.11), it must be true that

$$\left[\frac{\partial R(q_1^{NB}, 0, r_j^1, \mathbf{q^{NB}_{-1,2,j}})}{\partial q_j} - \frac{\partial T_j^{NB}(r_j^1)}{\partial q_j}\right]_- \geq 0 \tag{A.12}$$

where the notation $[\ ]_-$ indicates the left-hand derivative. Suppose the inequality in (A.12) is strict. Consider an arbitrarily small change in q_1 to $q_1^{NB} + x$. Since the marginal revenue function is continuous, the inequality in (A.12) will still hold at $r_j^1(q_1^{NB} + x, \mathbf{q^{NB}_{-1,j}})$. Therefore, $r_j^1(q_1^{NB}, \mathbf{q^{NB}_{-1,j}}) = r_j^1(q_1^{NB} + x, \mathbf{q^{NB}_{-1,j}})$. Suppose that (A.12) holds with equality. This means that the first-order condition holds for movements of q_j in the leftward direction. Movements in the rightward direction will not occur given small changes in marginal revenue because T_j^{NB} jumps upward in that direction. Analogous conditions hold for $r_j^2(q_1^{NB} + x, \mathbf{q^{NB}_{-2,j}})$.

Step 4. Suppose $T_j^{NB}(q_j)$ jumps up to the left of q_j^{NB}, but is continuous to the right. At the solution to (A.9), it must be true that

$$\left[\frac{\partial R(q_1^{NB}, 0, r_j^1, \mathbf{q^{NB}_{-1,2,j}})}{\partial q_j} - \frac{\partial T_j^{NB}(r_j^1)}{\partial q_j^1}\right]_+ \leq 0 \tag{A.13}$$

where $[\,]_+$ denotes the right hand derivative. Suppose the inequality in (A.13) is strict. By the same argument as in the preceding paragraph, a small change in q_1 to $q_1^{NB} + x$ will leave r_j^1 unchanged, i.e., $r_j^1(q_1^{NB}, \mathbf{q^{NB}_{-1,j}}) = r_j^1(q_1^{NB} + x, \mathbf{q^{NB}_{-1,j}})$. Suppose that (A.13) holds with equality. This means that the first-order condition holds for movements of q_j in the rightward direction. Movements in the leftward direction will not occur given small changes in marginal revenue because T_j^{NB} jumps upward in that direction. Analogous conditions hold for $r_j^2(q_1^{NB} + x, \mathbf{q^{NB}_{-2,j}})$.

Step 5. Steps 1-4 establish how the solution to each product's sub-maximization problem changes in response to small changes in q_1 starting at the equilibrium quantity q_1^{NB}. In particular, product j's quantity either does not change or it changes to satisfy its first order condition. We now establish that this is true for the solutions to the maximization problems in (A.9) and (A.10).

The solution to the problem in (A.9) is given by the simultaneous solution to the $N-2$ sub-maximization problems in (A.11). For a given change in q_1 to $q_1^{NB}+x$, let $\mathcal{S}$ be the subset of products for which the solution to the product's sub-maximization problem changes according to its first-order condition. By the implicit-function theorem, the simultaneous solution to the sub-maximization problems for products in $\mathcal{S}$ (holding constant the quantities of products not in $\mathcal{S}$) are continuous functions of q_1 on the interval $(q_1^{NB}, q_1^{NB}+x)$. This means that a small change x results in a small change in these quantities, and hence a small change in the marginal revenues of the other products whose sub-maximization solutions do not change in response to changes in q_1. Since the change in marginal revenue from all the adjustments for products in $\mathcal{S}$ is small, the quantities of the products not in $\mathcal{S}$ will not change in response to a small change in q_1 and the associated adjustments in quantities for products in $\mathcal{S}$. Therefore, in the solution to (A.9), the quantity q_j either does not respond to a small change in q_1, or it responds according to its first-order condition.

Now differentiate (23) in the text, and recognize that $\frac{\partial v_1(q_1^{NB})}{\partial q_1} = \frac{\partial R(q_1^{NB},0,\tilde{\mathbf{q}}_{-\mathbf{1},\mathbf{2}}(q_1^{NB}))}{\partial q_1}$ regardless of whether $T_j^{NB}(q_j)$ is smooth or continuous at q_j^{NB}. Proposition 3 follows as explained in the text. **Q.E.D.**

Proof of Proposition 4: We know from Propositions 1, 2, and 3 that the fully-integrated outcome is achieved pre and post merger if bundling is feasible or $\alpha_m < \overline{\alpha}_m$. In these cases, when there are no cost savings from the merger, the benefit to manufacturers 1 and 2 from merging is given by

$$\begin{aligned}\Delta\pi_m^B &= \pi_m^B - \pi_1^* - \pi_2^* \\ &= \alpha_m\left((\Pi - \Pi_{-1,2}) - (\Pi - \Pi_{-1}) - (\Pi - \Pi_{-2})\right). \qquad \text{(A.14)}\end{aligned}$$

To see that the right-hand side of (A.14) is positive, define

$$M(q_1, q_2) \equiv \max_{\mathbf{q_{-1,2}}} R(q_1, q_2, \mathbf{q_{-1,2}}) - w_1^I q_1 - w_2^I q_2 - \sum_{j \neq 1,2} w_j^I q_j. \tag{A.15}$$

Since the objective in (A.15) is concave in $(q_1, q_2, \mathbf{q_{-1,2}})$, it follows that M is concave in (q_1, q_2). Let $\tilde{q}_1 \equiv \arg\max_{q_1} M(q_1, 0)$ and $\tilde{q}_2 \equiv \arg\max_{q_2} M(0, q_2)$. Using these definitions along with the definitions of Π, $\Pi_{-1,2}$, Π_{-1}, and Π_{-2} in the text, we have

$$\begin{aligned}
\Pi - \Pi_{-1,2} &= M(q_1^I, q_2^I) - M(0,0) \text{ (by definition)} \\
&> [M(q_1^I, q_2^I) - M(0, q_2^I)] + [M(q_1^I, q_2^I) - M(q_1^I, 0)] \text{ (by concavity and uniqueness)} \\
&\geq [M(q_1^I, q_2^I) - M(0, \tilde{q}_2)] + [M(q_1^I, q_2^I) - M(\tilde{q}_1, 0)] \text{ (by the definition of } \tilde{q}_1 \text{ and } \tilde{q}_2) \\
&= (\Pi - \Pi_{-1}) + (\Pi - \Pi_{-2}) \text{ (by definition)},
\end{aligned}$$

which implies that the merger is profitable when bundling is feasible or $\alpha_m < \overline{\alpha}_m$.

If bundling is infeasible and $\alpha_m > \overline{\alpha}_m$, then Lemma 1 implies that constraints (19) and (20) will bind in any bargaining equilibrium. Suppose $\mathbf{q^{NB}} \equiv (q_1^{NB}, ..., q_N^{NB})$ and $\mathbf{T^{NB}} \equiv (T_1^{NB}, ..., T_N^{NB})$ form a bargaining equilibrium. Then, after some algebra, we can rearrange constraint (19) as

$$\begin{aligned}
F_1 &= R(\mathbf{q^{NB}}) - \sum_{j \neq 1,2} w_j^I q_j^{NB} - \left(\max_{q_{-1,2}} (R(0, q_2^{NB}, q_{-1,2}) - \sum_{j \neq 1,2} w_j^I q_j) \right) \\
&= R(\mathbf{q^{NB}}) - \sum_{j \neq 1} w_j^I q_j^{NB} - \left(\max_{q_{-1,2}} (R(0, q_2^{NB}, q_{-1,2}) - w_2^I q_2^{NB} - \sum_{j \neq 1,2} w_j^I q_j) \right) \\
&> R(\mathbf{q^{NB}}) - \sum_{j \neq 1} w_j^I q_j^{NB} - \left(\max_{q_{-1,2}} (R(0, q_2, q_{-1,2}) - w_2^I q_2 - \sum_{j \neq 1,2} w_j^I q_j) \right) \\
&= R(\mathbf{q^{NB}}) - \sum_{j \neq 1} w_j^I q_j^{NB} - \Pi_{-1},
\end{aligned} \tag{A.16}$$

where we have used the fact that the non-merging firms offer their products at marginal cost to the retailer whether or not bundling is feasible. Similarly, we can rearrange constraint (20) as

$$F_2 > R(\mathbf{q^{NB}}) - \sum_{j \neq 2} w_j^I q_j^{NB} - \Pi_{-2}. \tag{A.17}$$

It follows that the profit of merged firm when bundling is infeasible and $\alpha_m > \overline{\alpha}_m$ is

$$\pi_m^{NB} = F_1 + F_2 - C_m(q_1^{NB}, q_2^{NB})$$

$$> \sum_{i=1,2} \left(R(\mathbf{q^{NB}}) - \sum_{j \neq i} w_j^I q_j^{NB} - \Pi_{-i} \right) - C_m(q_1^{NB}, q_2^{NB})$$

$$> \sum_{i=1,2} \left(R(\mathbf{q^I}) - \sum_{j \neq i} w_j^I q_j^I - \Pi_{-i} \right) - C_m(q_1^I, q_2^I). \tag{A.18}$$

The first inequality follows from (A.16) and (A.17). The second inequality follows from the observation that the merged firm's profit increases when it induces the retailer to choose quantities $\mathbf{q^{NB}}$ rather than $\mathbf{q^I}$. Note that (A.18) corresponds to (34) in the text, as was to be proved. **Q.E.D.**

Proof of Proposition 6: Let $w_1^e(b)$ and $w_2^e(b)$ be the bargaining equilibrium wholesale prices for firms 1 and 2, respectively, and let $q_i^e(b)$, for all i, be the bargaining equilibrium quantities. Rearranging (38) and (39), the upstream profits for products 1 and 2 can be written as

$$\begin{aligned}
\pi_1 &= F_1 + w_1 q_1 - C_1(q_1) \\
&= R(\mathbf{q^e}(b)) - C_1(q_i^e(b)) - w_2^e(b) q_2^e(b) - \sum_{j \neq 1,2} w_j^I q_j^e(b) \\
&- \max_{\mathbf{q_{-1}}} \left(R(0, \mathbf{q_{-1}}) - w_2^e(b) q_2 - \sum_{j \neq 1,2} w_j^I q_j \right) + b,
\end{aligned} \tag{A.19}$$

$$\begin{aligned}
\pi_2 &= F_2 + w_2 q_2 - C_2(q_2) \\
&= R(\mathbf{q^e}(b)) - C_2(q_i^e(b)) - w_1^e(b) q_1^e(b) - \sum_{j \neq 1,2} w_j^I q_j^e(b) \\
&- \max_{\mathbf{q_{-2}}} \left(R(0, \mathbf{q_{-2}}) - w_1^e(b) q_1 - \sum_{j \neq 1,2} w_j^I q_j \right) + b.
\end{aligned} \tag{A.20}$$

Using (36), the profit of a rival firm i can be written as

$$\begin{aligned}
\pi_i &= \alpha_i [R(\mathbf{q^e}(b)) - C_i(q_i^e(b)) - w_1^e(b) q_1^e(b) - w_2^e(b) q_2^e(b) - \sum_{j \neq 1,2} w_j^I q_j^e(b) \\
&- \max_{\mathbf{q_{-1}}} \left(R(0, \mathbf{q_{-1}}) - w_1^e(b) q_1 - w_2^e(b) q_2 - \sum_{j \neq 1,2,i} w_j^I q_j \right)], \ \forall i \neq 1, \ 2.
\end{aligned} \tag{A.21}$$

Total profits can be written as

$$\pi = R(\mathbf{q^e}(b)) - \sum_i C_i(q_i^e(b)). \tag{A.22}$$

The retailer's profits are given by

$$\pi_r = \pi - \pi_1 - \pi_2 - \sum_{i \neq 1,2} \pi_i. \tag{A.23}$$

Let q_i^j maximize the retailer's profits when the retailer drops product j. For example, q_2^1 is the quantity of product 2 that solves the maximization term in equation (A.19). Substituting (A.19)-(A.22) into (A.23), differentiating π_r with respect to b, and using the envelope theorem gives

$$\frac{\partial \pi_r}{\partial b} = -2 - \left\{ \sum_{i \neq 1} \alpha_i (q_1^i - q_1^e) \frac{\partial w_1^e(b)}{\partial b} + \sum_{i \neq 2} \alpha_i (q_2^i - q_1^e) \frac{\partial w_2^e(b)}{\partial b} \right\}.$$

The terms involving $q_j^i - q_j^e$ for all i, $j \neq i$, are positive because the products are substitutes and an increase in b induces increases in w_1 and w_2. It follows that $\frac{\partial \pi_r}{\partial b} < 0$. **Q.E.D.**

REFERENCES

Adams, W. and J. Yellen (1976), "Commodity Bundling and the Burden of Monopoly," *Quarterly Journal of Economics*, 90: 474-498.

Bernheim, D. and M. Whinston (1985), "Common Marketing Agency as a Device for Facilitating Collusion," *Rand Journal of Economics*, 15: 269-281.

Bernheim, D. and M. Whinston (1998), "Exclusive Dealing," *Journal of Political Economy*, 106: 64-103.

Bertrand, J. (1883), "Theorie Mathematique de la Richesse Sociale," *Journal des Savants*, 67: 499-508.

Carlton, D. and M. Waldman (2002), "The Strategic Use of Tying to Preserve and Create Market Power in Evolving Industries," *Rand Journal of Economics*, 33: 194-220.

Choi, J. and C. Stefanadis (2001), "Tying, Investment, and the Dynamic Leverage Theory," *Rand Journal of Economics*, 32: 52-71.

Colangelo, G. (1995), "Vertical vs. Horizontal Integration: Pre-Emptive Merging," *Journal of Industrial Economics*, 43: 323-337; and correction, 45: 115.

Cournot, A. (1838), *Recherches sur les Principes Mathematiques de la Theorie des Richesses*, Paris: Hachette, 1838. (English translation by N. T. Bacon published in Economic Classics [Macmillan, 1897] and reprinted in 1960 by Augustus M. Kelly.)

Davidson, C (1988) "Multiunit Bargaining in Oligopolistic Industries," *Journal of Labor Economics*, 6: 397-422.

Deneckere, R. and C. Davidson (1985), "Incentives to Form Coalitions with Bertrand Competition," *Rand Journal of Economics*, 16: 473-486.

Dobson, P. and M. Waterson, (1997), "Countervailing Power and Consumer Prices," *Economic Journal*, 107: 418-430.

Farrell, J. and C. Shapiro (1990), "Horizontal Mergers: An Equilibrium Analysis," *American Economic Review*, 80: 107-126.

Horn H. and A. Wolinsky (1988), "Bilateral Monopolies and Incentives for Mergers," *Rand Journal of Economics*, 19: 408-419.

Inderst, R. and C. Wey (2003), "Bargaining, Mergers, and Technology Choice in Bilaterally Oligopolistic Industries," *Rand Journal of Economics*, 34: 1-19.

Jun, B., "Non-cooperative Bargaining and Union Formation," *The Review of Economic Studies*, 56: 59-76.

Mathewson, F. and R. Winter (1997), "Tying as a Response to Demand Uncertainty," *Rand Journal of Economics*, 28: 566-573.

McAfee, P, McMillan, J. and M. Whinston (1989), "Multiproduct Monopoly, Commodity Bundling, and Correlation of Values," *Quarterly Journal of Economics*, 104: 371-384.

McAfee, R.P. and M. Schwartz (1994), "Opportunism in Multilateral Vertical Contracting: Nondiscrimination, Exclusivity, and Uniformity," *American Economic Review*, 84: 210-230.

O'Brien, D.P. and G. Shaffer (1992), "Vertical Control with Bilateral Contracts," *Rand Journal of Economics*, 23: 299-308.

O'Brien, D. P. and G. Shaffer (1994), "The Welfare Effects of Forbidding Discriminatory Discounts: A Secondary Line Analysis of Robinson-Patman," *Journal of Law, Economics and Organization*, 10: 296-318.

O'Brien, D. P. and G. Shaffer (1997), "Nonlinear Supply Contracts, Exclusive Dealing, and Equilibrium Market Foreclosure," *Journal of Economics and Management Strategy*, 6: 755-85.

Salant, S., Switzer, S. and R. Reynolds (1983), "Losses From Horizontal Merger: the Effects of an Exogenous Change in Industry Structure on Cournot-Nash Equilibrium," *Quarterly Journal of Economics*, 98: 185-199.

Shaffer, G. (1991), "Capturing Strategic Rent: Full-Line Forcing, Brand Discounts, Aggregate Rebates, and Maximum Resale Price Maintenance," *Journal of Industrial Economics*, 39: 557-75.

Stigler, G. (1964), "A Theory of Oligopoly," *Journal of Political Economy*, 72: 44-61.

Tom, W., Balto, D., and N. Averitt (2000), "Anticompetitive Aspects of Market-Share Discounts and Other Incentives to Exclusive Dealing," *Antitrust Law Journal*, 67: 615-639.

Von Ungern-Sternberg, T. (1996), "Countervailing Power Revisited," *International Journal of Industrial Organization*, 14: 507-520.

Whinston, M. (1990), "Tying, Foreclosure, and Exclusion," *American Economic Review*, 80: 837-859.

Willig, R. (1991), "Merger Analysis, Industrial Organization Theory, and Merger Guidelines," *Brookings Papers on Economic Analysis*, Microeconomics Issue, 281-332.

Ziss, S. (1995), "Vertical Separation and Horizontal Mergers," *Journal of Industrial Economics*, 43: 63-75.

www.ingramcontent.com/pod-product-compliance
Lightning Source LLC
Chambersburg PA
CBHW081241170526
45165CB00009B/3150
* 9 7 8 1 5 0 2 5 2 4 3 1 7 *